An Illustrated Poetry Collection

SPACE COW

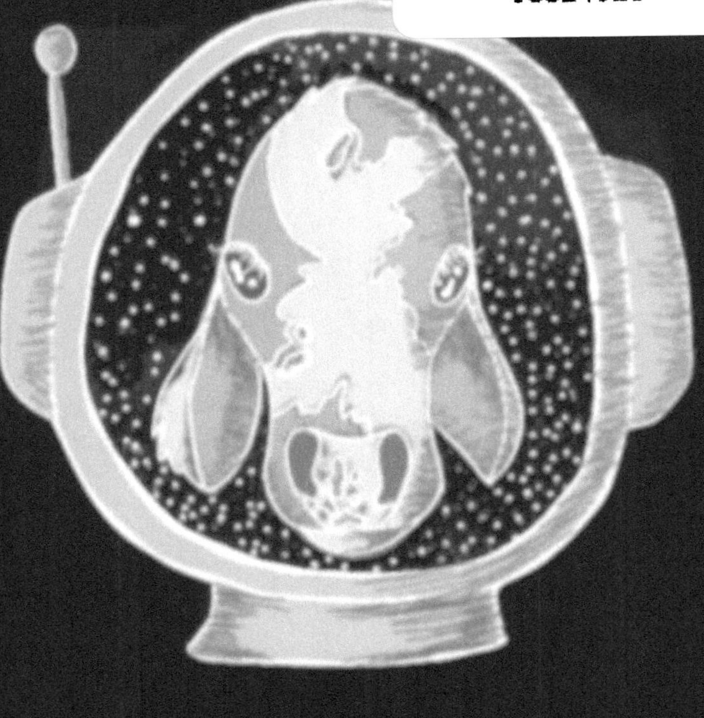

LO BELLAFONT

SPACE COW

AN ILLUSTRATED POETRY COLLECTION

LO BELLAFONT

Cover Illustration by Lo Bellafont

Interior Design by Mafia Moon Designs

Interior Illustration by Lo Bellafont

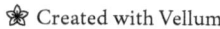 Created with Vellum

CONTENTS

For those who experience life, a little to the left.

Part One:
The Storytellers

MILKYWAY

There once was a cow, who lived on a farm by the bay,
She grew tired of the same fields
And the same barn every day,

Until she leapt from a sea cliff,
Not knowing how to swim,
And with no wings to lift.

So, God flipped the world upside down,
And she landed among the stars;

Now she bounds from planet to planet every night,
Without any sort of stress or plight

And although the earth is upside down to this day,
You can still look into the night sky,
And see her Milkyway.

BIG BLACK HOUNDS

The big black hounds they howl on the shore,
Howl on the shore.
Yes, the big black hounds they howl on the shore,
Waiting for the masters to return home.

The big black hounds they protect the master's wives,
Protect the master's wives.
Yes, the big black hounds they protect the master's wives,
As the storms rage.

For the sailors they are away at sea,
Are away at sea.
Yes, the sailors they are away at sea,
Fishing far from the harbor.

The poor stray cats they yowl for more milk,
Yowl for more milk.
Yes, the poor stray cats, they yowl for more milk,
For the fishing boats never came.

The big black hounds they chase away the little stray cats,

Chase away the little stray cats.
Yes, the big black hounds chase away the little stray cats,
So, they don't steal any food.

The wives they mourn with their sons and daughters,
With their sons and daughters.
Yes, the wives mourn with their sons and daughters,
As the hounds wait.

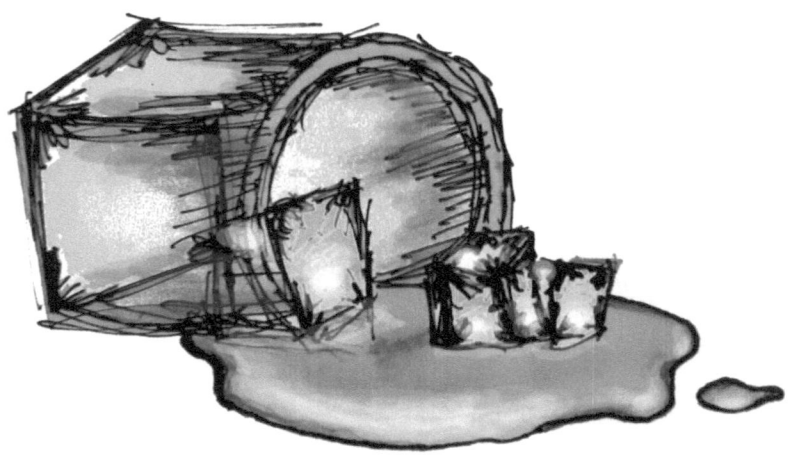

WHO DONE IT?

There is a castle on the coast,
Inside there is a party,
Of which a wealthy man hosts

Then he is murdered in the banquet hall
Now all his guests just awkwardly stand around
Wondering who will be the next to fall.

A wraith of theories and rumors
Already begin to zig-zag throughout the hushed group,
Trying to figure out which of them
Would be so low to stoop.

With unfinished drinks in hand,
The germ of distrust passes to another pair of eager lips
Uttering's of betrayal, between hesitant sips.

The authorities were called about an hour ago,
But because of the blizzard outside, nobody came.
After this night, the remaining would never be the same.

TRIAL AND TRIBULATION

Two mules saunter down a dusted road,
Trial and Tribulation they are called.
One brown, the other grey,
Both come to bring destruction today.
Behind them they carry a wagon
Filled with broken dreams.
The two mules, not as innocent as they seem.

Trial and Tribulation stomp on the farmlands
crushing homes beneath their hooves.
They knock rocks and boulders down the cliff side
Then steal the remaining loaves.
The families left hungry and homeless
Without their bread or roofs.

Once finished with their selfish play
Trial and Tribulation disappear into the desert.
Kicking up dust and pushing through the sage
To the next little town, they roam.

THREE PURPLE FOXTAILS

There once was a fox,
Born being chased by three horrible fails.

On the day she became too tired
To keep running from them,
She realized they were nothing more,
Than her three purple tails.

But the other foxes were not as surprised.
In fact, they kept chasing her, until early sunrise.

"Change your terrible tails and be like us!"
They had yelled all through the night.
Even at daybreak, chanting it with all of their might.

Before leaving that meadow for good, to find a new home,
The timid purple fox uttered a reply, as brave as she could.

"There are many you's in this world.
Like you and you and you and you and you,

But there is only one me.
So being not-you, is all I will be."

THE WINEMAKER

Down in the valley,
In columns of vibrant green,
Nestle the purple fruits of his labor,
Of which the wise would be keen

For years, he toiled
Fending off birds that picked
And snakes that coiled.
Timing everything just right.

When they're ready he harvests them
By the baskets full, but it's still not complete.
He then marches round and round,
Squishing them with his feet.

Once the juice is all pressed out,
It's time to stir in the yeast,
And they ferment in wooden cylinders,
Hidden from a thirsty world and its feasts.

When the process is all finished,

The Winemaker smiles with pride,
He bottles up his indigo gold.
The thick sour liquid served to groom and bride.

When one takes that first sniff,
And then puckers their lips at the edge
Of the glass, for that first sip,
They can't help but savor every last drip.

Silently they thank the Lord, and praise the Winemaker

FIALOVA

His friends asked him
What ever happened
To his first love?
He parted his lips, with a sigh
And this was his reply:
Her name was Fialova.
Her eyes would enchant me still.
And though I missed her so so much,
I'm glad she didn't keep in touch, because
I see
I no longer need her.
I hope that doesn't sound mean,
But, what I mean is,
I've learned to live without her eyes
Her pretty laugh, her sweet sweet lies.
I had to move on, when she moved along.

His first love found him once again
And reached out
Asking if he would like to try again.
He pressed down the tip of his quill,

With a sigh,
And this was his reply:
My first darling Fialova
Your eyes would enchant me still.
And though I missed you so so much
I'm glad we didn't keep in touch, because
I see,
I no longer need you.
I hope that doesn't sound mean, but
What I mean is,
I've learned to live without your eyes
Your facade laugh, your deceiving lies.
I had to move on, when you moved along.

After he rejected his first love's second letter
And ignored her third.
He asked his new Amore,
What she thought of the situation.
She parted her lips
With a sigh
And this was her reply:
Your first darling Fialova,
She gave you such a thrill.
And though you missed her so so much,
I'm glad you didn't keep in touch, because,
I see, she's a part of the life, that made you,
Into the man, you are now.
But now, you're a man who belongs to me.
And I don't plan to ever move along.
And he replied
With a smile
And I don't plan to ever move on.

A few nights later

There was a knock
At their apartment door
And when they opened it together,
His first darling Fialova,
Stumbled back in shock.
For she had grown even more stubborn,
And she would die on this hill.
With a gasp
She parted her lips,
And this was her greeting:

Oh darling,
how I've missed you so, so much!
I've tried so hard to keep in touch!
Why have you been so *mean*?
Can't you see
That I still *need* you?
But you've made it clear,
I'm no longer the one that you hold dear!
Why are people always moving along?
Oh why can't I ever move on?

8

A PET FIT FOR A PIRATE PRINCE

Lupe sat in the belly of his father's ship,
The contents of his belly,
Swaying with the waves and gurgling with every dip.

That's when he looked up to the sound of boots
Trop trop trop, down the stairs.

The door swung open
To reveal the captain, a pillager of loots

"Lupe my boy! I've got you something!"
The captain jollied

With a beady look in his eyes,
Holding something behind his back

He slowly revealed, a little glass critter trap
With a woman from the Mayfly Kingdom inside.

Lupe's eyes widened; he had never seen a live Mayfly.
For his father's crew hunted them to near extinction

(The land folk loved to turn their wings
Into jewelry and decoration).

The captain tossed the trap,
And Lupe lurched forward to catch it.
But the Mayfly had fallen back,

Now she was upside down
And pressed against the opposite wall of the trap.

She pulled her ringlet curls out of the way,
Revealing a powerful little glare on her face.

Then she got herself turned around and upright
With dignity and grace.

Lupe could see her leotard-like clothing
Was made from flower petals.
She stretched out her wings to straighten them out,

And Lupe marveled at them
Like the most precious of metals.

Stitched together with spider web
It was like thin intersecting crystals.

In the sharp tails were designs
That looked like flat human eyes.

And when they fluttered
They hummed like a harp.

And they seemed to faze
In and out of reality

With the way they reflected the light,
One moment almost completely clear,

The next, shining with the brilliant
Colors of the northern lights.
Leaving poor Lupe in a daze

With a satisfied laugh,
The captain left Lupe alone, with his new pet

Closing the door,
Before letting in a draft.

Once he knew they were alone
Lupe quickly got up and opened a window,

Sunshine cascaded through
And a chilling breeze came in with a moan

Then he got out his knife
And began to pick at the lock on the trap

When it finally popped open, Lupe sat back,
And gestured toward the window

"You're free! You have to go!"
"Please…. before my father comes back."

For it was a life of cages
He wanted her to lack

The Mayfly's eyes were wide,
And her tiny pink lips quivered.

She crawled frantically out of the trap, and onto the table.
She tried flapping her wings, With a frown

And they glowed as she shakily hovered for a moment,
Before they flickered, and she fell back down.

"What's wrong? Are you hurt?"
Lupe leaned forward.

She looked up at him,
And pressed her hands to her stomach.

Lupe squinted and saw he could see her ribs,
And she longingly looked over with a sigh

At the still warm bowl of broth and noodles nearby.
"Oh," He grabbed the spoon

"You're hungry"
And carefully brought it in front of the Mayfly, "here."

She stood on her toes of tip
And placed her hands at the edge of the spoon

To steady it and herself.
She angled her head down and began to sip.

The Mayfly pulled away to take a breath,
Her cheeks flushed from the heat,

Her body becoming filled
With nourishment and serenity.

Lupe stirred the broth

So he could see the different ingredients bob up.

He scooped a bit of bok choy,
Mushroom, red pepper, rice noodle, green onion, and carrots

The Mayfly excited at the sights
Picking at and munching on the pieces,

Taking sips of the broth
In between the bites.

When she was finished
She took a few steps back, looking satisfied.

The Mayfly reached for her side, but saw that nothing
Was in her belt made of vines.

Then she looked into the trap
And pulled out what looked like a tiny needle.

Though small, in that moment she looked as mighty,
As the mightiest lord, and Lupe chuckled,
"It appears you're going to need a bigger sword."

9

THE SEA MAIDEN

Little Adelaide, age six
Wrapped up in her favorite blanket,
Goes out onto the porch with a cup of coco.
The world is a hazy, glittering grey,
From the morning sea mist.

She looks up at her father,
She's such an itty bitty thing next to him,
And he a protective sentinel beside her,
She asks him
"Pa, where does the mist come from?"

"It comes from the sea,
The wind carries it from the ocean to the shore."
He answers, his deep voice climbing through his beard
To be met with briny frigid air in a crystalized puff.
"But why? How?" Adelaide asks.

He smiles down at her,
Squinty eyes barely glinting beneath beanie.
He sits down on the steps of the porch,

And gestures to the space beside,
And she sits down with curious eyes.

"Let me tell you a story, Addie,"
He begins, looking wistfully out
Into the silvery nothing,
Knowing instinctively
Where the sand meets ocean in the distance.

"There was once a pirate, and he led his crew
With an iron fist,
He only had a soft spot,
For his rambunctious daughter.
On his death bed, he made her Captain.

But the crew, did not want to listen
To the command of a woman.
They pretended to hold her word in high esteem
For a while, out of respect for the dead man.
But just like love, you can't hide hatred forever.

So, they conspired, and threw her overboard
Into the dark, cold waves.
Most wouldn't have survived,
But you see, her father taught her the ways of the sea,
She knew her like a mother.

She fought until slits in her neck
And in between her ribs opened up,
And the salt water began rushing in through them,
Her eyes shot open, now hardened, and lit up like embers.
And with the new webbing that stretched between her fingers,
She swam up to the surface.

The water inside her, transformed into mist
And got expelled into the air all around her.
She could breathe! In an entirely new way.
She swore she would help other women
Tossed about by the hand of man.

You see Addie, the mist all around us,
That visits with every sunrise,
Is the breath of women,
That men tried but could not drown.
Shouting, singing, *"I'm still here!"*

THRALL OF THE RAT KING

A young rat of pleasant manner
By the name of Salty Cracker
Decided to leave the surface of the city
And all its uptown glamor.

Down into the sewers he scurried and trudged
Through the waste and over the sludge
To find more of his kind
Leaving the life of a loner behind.

That's when he came across another,
A rat named Cookie Crumb
Who took him in like a mother,
And she led him to her clan that hid from the sun.

They welcomed Salty Cracker with open paws
Bestowing him with gifts, and even applause.
Which was odd to Salty Cracker,
He hadn't accomplished anything worthy of this.

As the days passed by, (or was it nights?
It was hard to tell the time down here)
The clan taught him the way of enlightenment
"We must all tie our tails together tight!"

Salty Cracker didn't like that idea.

So, he chuckled awkwardly, and bid them farewell
They made expressions
Like he had just said something odd,
Or they had smelt an awful smell.

"No Salty Cracker, you're one of us now.
One of us
One of us
One of us

Stay with your new family,
Stay in your new home.
Who else will you bond with?
Where else will you go?

Don't you want to feel a connection so strong?"
So, they grabbed Salty Cracker,
And sang him their Rat King song.
He fought, and he fought,

But *oh*, they were *right*,
Knotting their tails together
It just felt so right.
It was like they formed a brand-new creature

It put him on a cerebral high ground.

And the idea of leaving it all,
Caused a fear, a *sting*, that was visceral.
Over time, his sanity slipped, and his brain washed away.

Succumbing to the thrall of the Rat King.

Part Two:
The Sappy

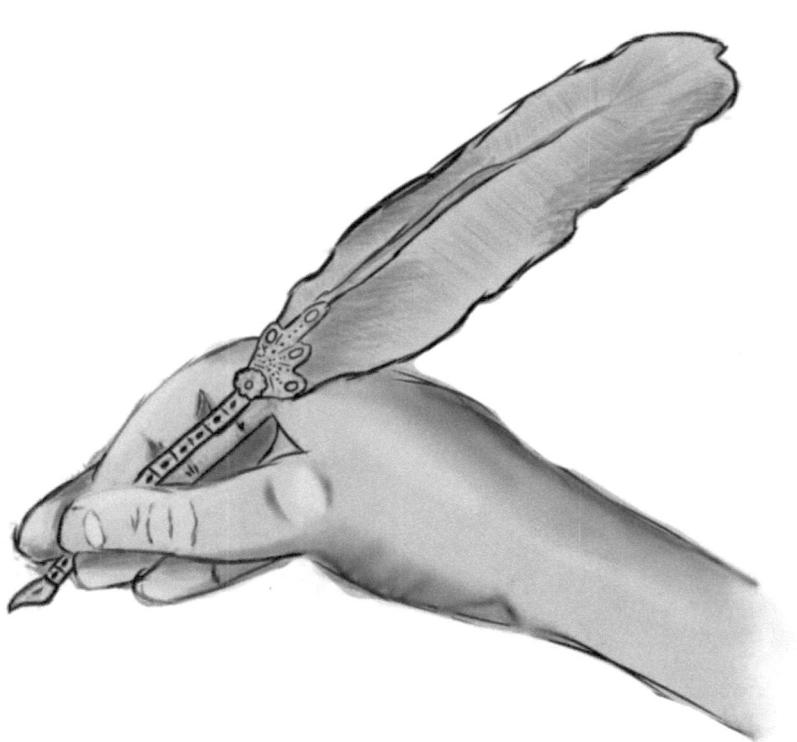

MY FAVORITE WORDS

Dawdling – To slowly wander
Flummoxed – Confused after too much to ponder
Plethora – When numbered amounts go beyond yonder
Your Name – There is no word of which, that I am fonder.

PLUTO

If you asked me if I loved you to the moon,
I'd say don't park my rocket so soon,
My love for you goes even beyond the blue of Neptune.
I love you to Pluto and back.

SEASONS

When the horizon wiggles
From the immensity of the heat
And the public pools fill with giggles

When deciduous arbors are drained of their chlorophyll
And school bells blare once more
And water park rides stand still

When snow finds its way down from space
And reaches up to grab hold of its fellow flakes
And swing them down into place

When tulips fizzle beneath the white
And pop up like buttered toast
Dotting the hills that shimmer with new light

That's when I'll be loving you most.

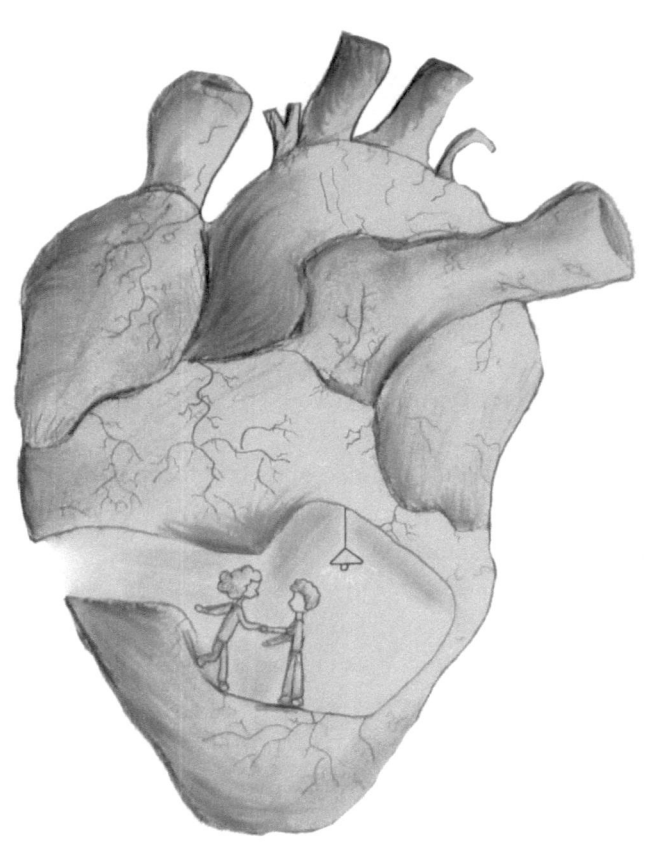

BEFORE

Our friendship has meant
So *much* to me, for so *long*,
I can't even remember what it's like
to not have you so deep in my heart.
I pity my past self,
Oh, the emptiness
She must have felt in her chest,
Before there was you.

HOW YOU MAKE ME FEEL

Darlin'
You put the moon in my chest

HER PRAYER

"Oh Lord
Does he talk to you about me?

Like I talk to you,
About him?"

THE WEIGHT OF LOVE

When I first started loving you
It made me feel *light*

Like a ballerina tenderly dancing in a meadow,
Impossibly not bending
The flowers beneath her toes.

But now some time has passed,
And the burden of keeping my love under secrecy
Has grown rather heavy.

And I feel like an awkward monster
Loud and embarrassed, trying not to be obvious,
Trampling over
And crushing the trees of a forest.

18

FORGET ME NOTS

I oughta' leave Forget-Me-Nots
At your doorstep,
And in your pockets,
And under your pillow.
And tuck a stem behind your ear like a pencil.
And envelop their dried petals in resin
To make jewelry for you to wear.

Just for the chance
To leave an imprint on your mind.

For I know we've known each other for far too long
For me to be a new and exciting part of your life,
It's okay, if I'm just a tiny flower
In the winding landscape of your world.

But even if you never grow
To feel the same way about me,
Wherever you go,
Whatever you do,

Whoever you end up with,
Know that you and our friendship
Mean so much to me,

So *please*
Don't forget about little old me.

19

FLOWER CHILD

If a piece of me
Turned into flower,
Every time love
Grew inside my heart

Then my spine would turn into stem,
Skin into leaf
Freckles into pollen
Hair into vine.

Eyelids into petals
Tooth and nail into thorn
Nerves into roots
Organs into fruit

Sweat into nectar
Tears into wine
Blood into tea
Stomach acid, brewed into poison

Feelings threaded into rainbows

Thoughts into the buzzing of bees
Memory into the humming of birds
Dreams into the flittering of white moths

I would leave a trail of soil wherever I go
And children would scream
And old women would hold up their crosses
At such a hideous thing

And I would continue loving still.

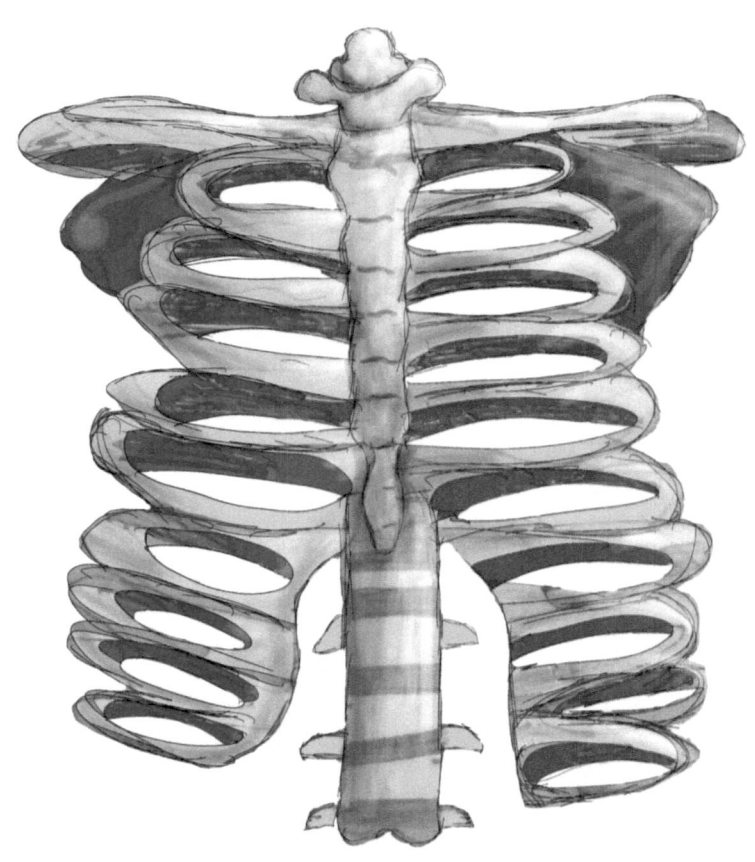

20

RIBCAGE

I don't just love you with my whole heart
I love you with my whole chest.

But all of these feelings for you,
All of this respect
And trust
And admiration
And wonder
And comfort
And excitement
And affection

Are locked up inside of my ribcage,
And I seem to have misplaced the key.

Part Three:
The Satirical

TEA WITH DRAGONS

Having tea with dragons is rather difficult,
Because they always manage to spill.
Having dinner with dragons leaves me fuming,
Because they never split the bill.
Ballroom dancing with dragons is a feat,
Because they have such big ones.
Reading with dragons is a challenge,
Since their breath burns like the sun.
Swimming with dragons would be silly,
Since they don't like to get their wings wet.
Can't take a dragon to the theater
Or the actors would surely fret.
Can't keep a dragon as a pet,
Or I would become a tasty meal.

But still,
I wish dragons were real.

THE ULTIMATE GRILLED CHEESE SANDWHICH

Two slices of sourdough,
Now spread tart cherry jam to and fro.
Have some turkey piled on,
And then mozzarella, thick as the walls of Babylon.
After you grill it all together, eating it is next,
Then you'll see this sandwich is better than…

THINGS I AM GRATEFUL FOR

1. There are wonderful people in my life

2. Beavers aren't carnivores

IF I HAD A BOAT

If you had a boat, what would its name be?
I'd call mine the 'Not A Car'
But the 'Not' would be spelled like Nautical.
So it would be the 'Nautacar'
With it I would sail the Italian Riviera.
And also I would visit your boat.

This isn't really a poem
Just a thought.

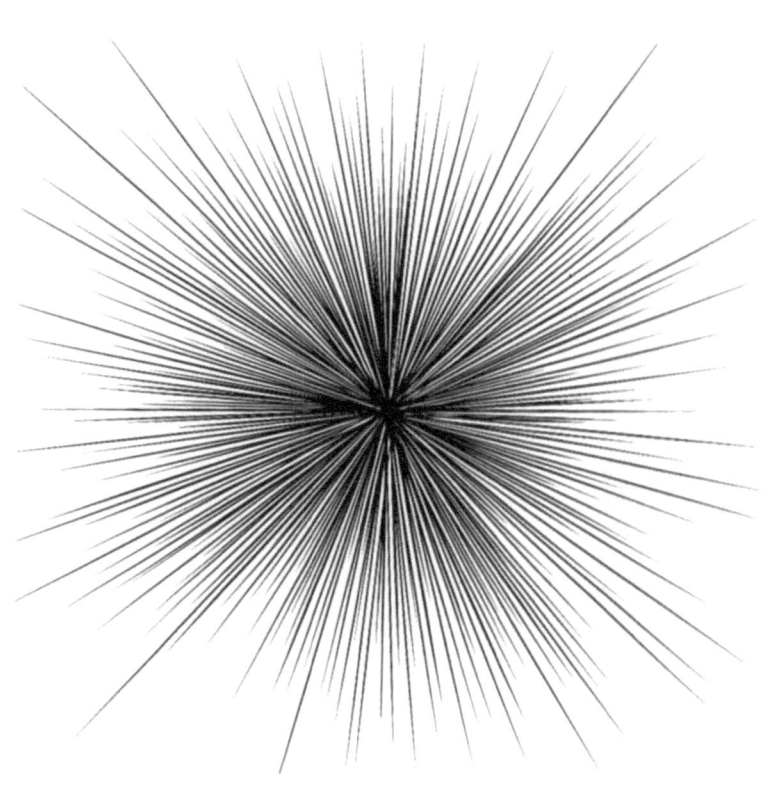

THINGS THAT I THINK ARE COOL

Lightning, power ripping open the sky,
Only chased by the brave,
Bioluminescence, a chemical reaction
That makes a glowing cave.
Echolocation, sound bouncing back to its original place,
Black Holes, gravity at its greatest so far out in space.

You, with that complex mind and wonderful face

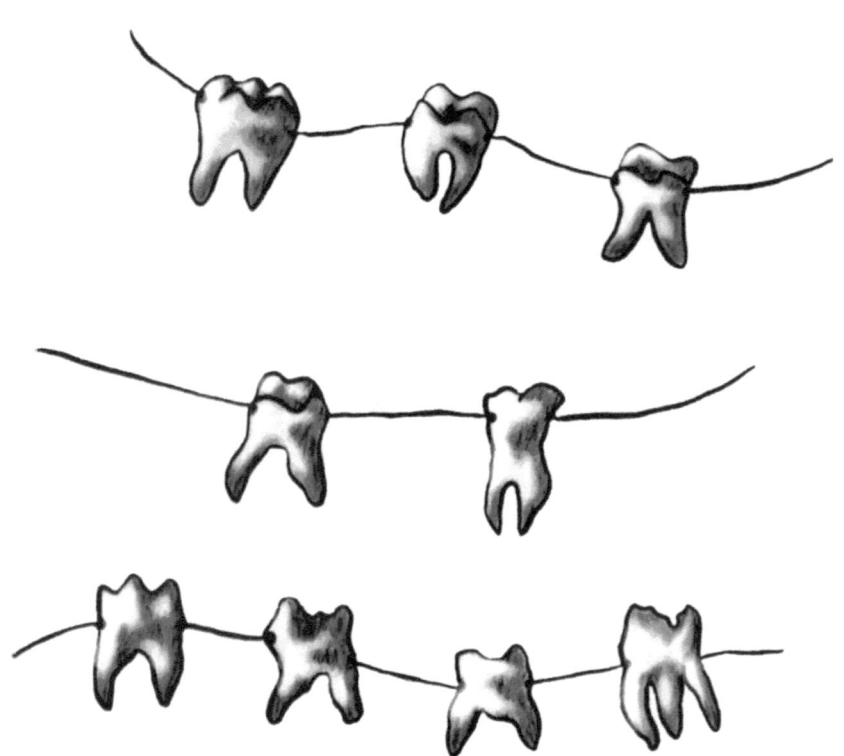

TURN ME LOOSE

When I'm old and senile,
Don't put me in a home
Turn me loose in the woods
And just let me roam.

Do not preserve me,
I'm not art,
Do not praise me,
I'm not smart.

Let me wander aimlessly
Pass tree and wild rose,
Head pointed up at the stars
With a frost bit nose.

Let my bones creak brittle,
Let me bathe in a brook,
Don't take me to a hospital,
I'll make a cave my special nook.

I'll giggle at the voices,

And reach for the faces,
Faltering peacefully
Aging with grace.

I'll frolic through a meadow,
As memory of the life before, fades away
Forgetting all of the stress,
Happily confused to greet each day.

I'll live off of berries and mushrooms,
And fish, and squirrels.
Off of pine needle tea,
And roots and blooms.

No one would ask me to lend a hand,
For I would lend them three.
If anyone asked for my string of pearls,
I'd give them my string of teeth.

I'll find a nice river
To lay down by.
I'll rot safe and sound,
On moss covered ground,

And let out my last sigh.

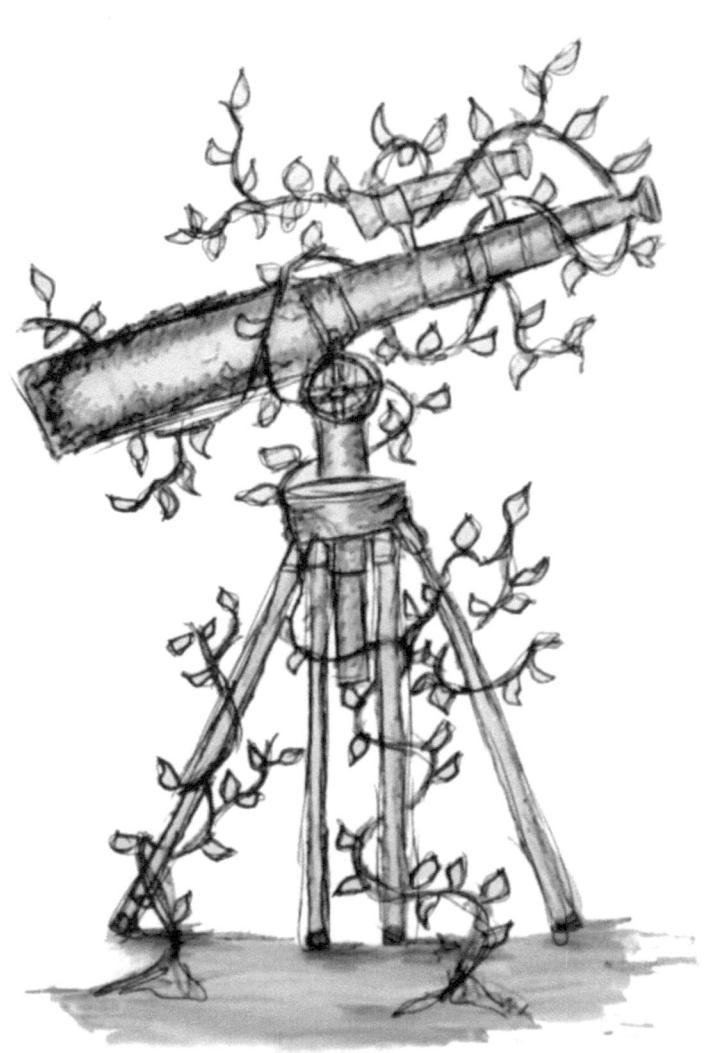

CHARTING TREES

Do you think aliens chart our trees?
Like we chart their stars?
Soaring over our Earth,
With telescopes pointed *down*.

Connecting the dots and creating pictures
With their hive-mind,
For they travel like the bees.
Do you think they create maps of the forests,
All the way from Mars?
Do you think they believe the shapes and sizes
Have special meaning?
Or do I sound like a clown?

Just think for a moment if you please,
Succumb to imagination, forget your smarts.
And believe for a moment, that aliens are just like us.
Simple and curious and creative, and chart the trees of our
ground.

FRISK

Welcome to the town of Frisk.
A town of wooden dolls, left up in the attic,
Long after the scorn of a fire
Laid her black and dusty kisses on the walls
And the wealthy family downstairs.

The mayor of Frisk dawdles
Around the dollhouse of little late Anne-Marie,
Watching out the plastic window,
At the cardboard boxes turned into homes
"Why don't they build themselves such pretty furniture as
mine?"

And in his gloating,
His rotund belly bloating,
He sees a Russian figurine
With a Russian figure
And he raises his eyebrow
In greedy curiosity.

He has himself a proper bed,

Has himself his own porcelain tea-set
And matching porcelain wife.
Until her shattered remains
Crash down the stairs late into the night.

In his "grief" he needs new companionship,
So, he falls at the feet of the Russian doll,
Pleading for her affection.
She wants a break, from the wounds eaten by mold,
The cracked ceramic from being ripped by frost and cold.

So, she agrees, and takes his hand
And makes him promise, to send
Their greatest men, to search for resources
Outside the attic, to fairly share
With the poor among them.

Does the mayor of Frisk keep his promise?
Just because his heart is made from tree bone
And imagination, does it not have any compassion inside?
Or does it only beat with pride?
He makes excuses, for he likes the way life is now.

The Russian doll, (did he even ever ask her name?)
Weds atop the old vanity, a couple of the bulbs
Still thrumming with amber glow
Oblivious to her new husband's easy justifications.
Will she too forget the plea and poverty of her fellow doll?

Years pass and she guiltily chugs the wine of wealth
In the left-wing tower of the dollhouse,
In a bathtub with make-believe suds,
Wondering where she went wrong?
Another fight with the husband, who said he'd cure all.

That's when she sees a cat
Outside the big glass window,
Shivering in the winter winds.
She gives her husband a perfume la fish.
As a gift, bidding for his trust and forgiveness

She sneaks out that night
And treks across the attic, glared at
By the people she promised to save.
And she climbs to unlock the window.
Pushing it open with all of her might.

And the cat with stray eyes, more fiery
Than that of the dancing heat that took the lives
Of its owners, many a year ago.
It leaps across the land of the doll
Up and over the cardboard houses.

She swallows the mayor of Frisk.

HOMELESS STAN

There once was a homeless man
In a hopeless land, named Homeless Stan.
And he liked to feed the pigeons.
The pigeons they all fell down.
Raining from the sky, all through town.
Because World War Three, came early.
But Homeless Stan would not give up,
For as long as he lived he would cheer his friends up.
Even though all his friends would turn to dust,
In the nuclear holocaust.

30

CHLORINE

There are seven sad clowns
Outside my motel room
They sit around the pool
With their feet dipped in.

The turquoise glow
Illuminates their black and white faces
And Avant-garde pajamas,
Under the rolling dark of the summer night sky

There is a pungent ache pulsing in my temple
And my tongue is a sultry sour thing,
And my bladder hangs heavy in my pelvis,
And I think the chlorine, might be getting to me.

Part Four:
The Sorrowful

31

DEPRESSION

It takes so much time
And *energy*
To climb out of the pit,

That a lot of times
It just feels easier
To stay down here

And wait,
For the earth to swallow me whole;

But it *is* possible

The Lord may not remove the pit,
But He'll lower a rope down

And give you the courage
To hold on tight.

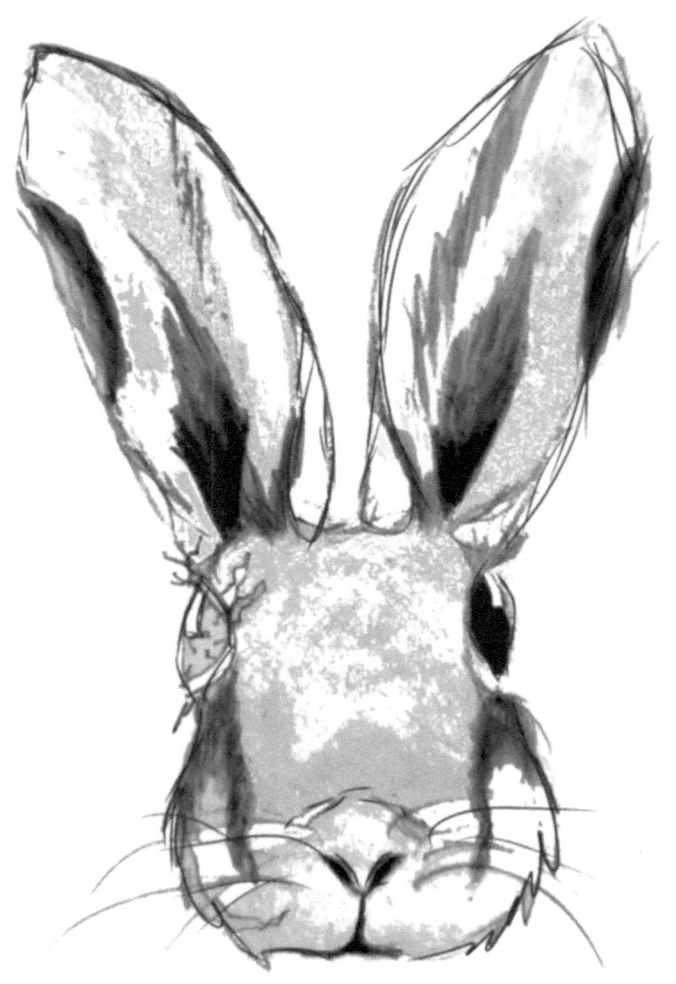

32

ANXIETY

You can't catch the rabbit, if the rabbit's deep underground.
You can't catch the culprit, if they're in jail safe and sound.
You can't catch the monster, if the monster isn't around.

But sometimes the rabbit, isn't a saint.
But sometimes culprits, can unlock the gate.
But sometimes the Monster, is just running late.

ELEPHANT'S PARASITE

Sometimes I feel like my voice doesn't matter,
Like my thoughts are not that of a person,
But of a parasite inside of an elephant's brain.

So, when things don't go right,
Or I am suffering inside,
I simply bite my tongue and smile,

Because I am not the elephant
I am just its annoyance
I couldn't possibly bend its will.

But what if this elephant is blind,
And I am watching through its hollow eyes,
As it strolls towards a cliff?

ENOUGH

I am not cruel; I am not evil.
I know I am good enough to be loved.

But am I interesting enough to be *noticed?*
Strong enough to be *useful?*
Smart enough to *succeed?*
Brave enough to *matter?*

Will "Good," ever feel *good enough?*

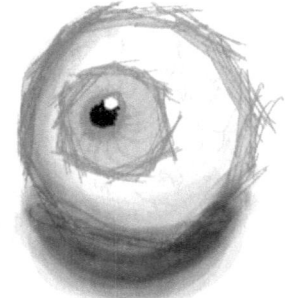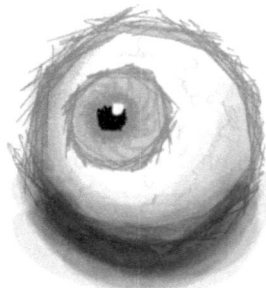

GET OUT

Why must my eyes scream

Get out
Get out
GET OUT

While my heart cries

Hold me
Hold me
HOLD ME

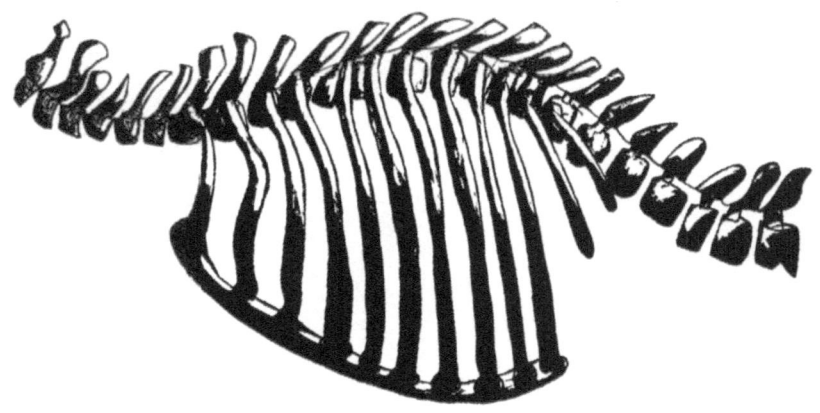

WHY I LOVE

My weak heart aches
For your wellbeing,
And my weak spine shakes
As I cry
To know,
You don't even see *why*.

EBB AND FLOW

Time is an omnipresent black sea
And the present is a pillar of salt I stand upon.
Another rises in front of me,
I must step onto it if I am to extend my life.
As the one before crumbles away into the abysmal past.

Sometimes I wish I could pause and rest,
On the top of an especially forgiving cylinder.
Or skip through twenty,
To a more exciting hour.
But I cannot slow or speed the ebb and flow.

I can pick a direction for the salt to grow
But I must stick to this preset pace,
And wait to see what's to come.
I am ever stepping away from my birth
Into the unknown.

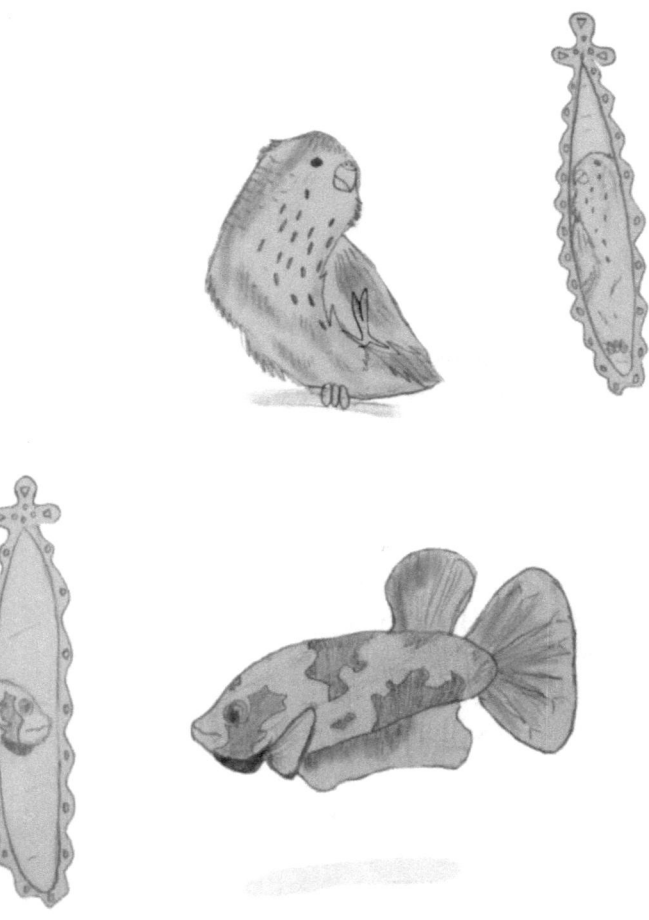

38

BETTA AND BUDGIE

There's a Betta in my brain
And he flares nonstop
Because my skull is made of mirror
I fear this Betta's 'bout to pop

There's a Budgie in my brain
And he flirts nonstop
Because my skull is made of mirror
I fear this Budgie's 'bout to drop

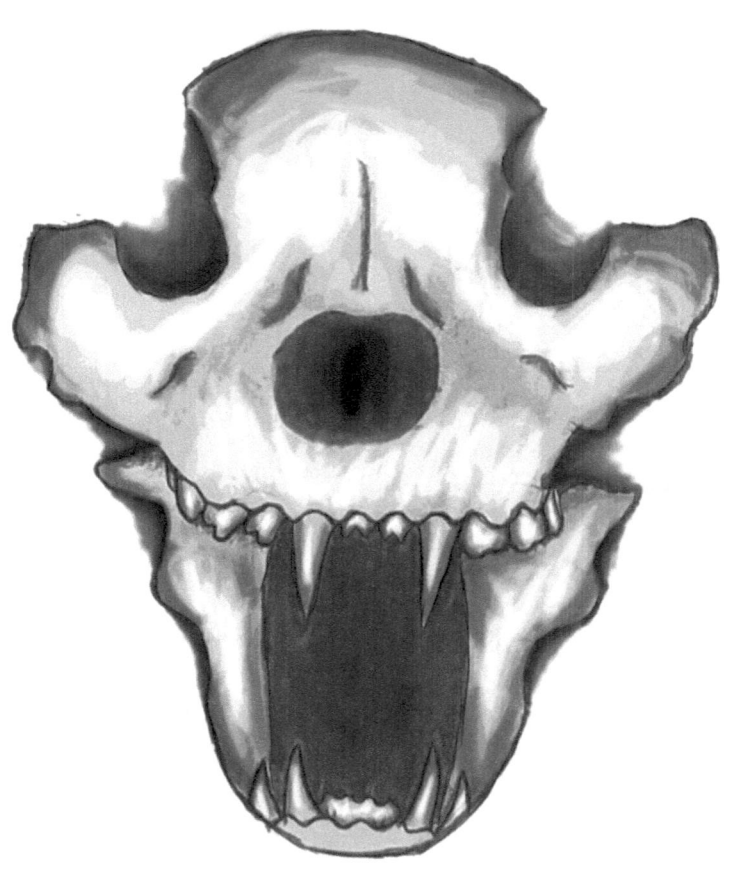

39

GIRLHOOD

I've been screaming screaming screaming through the silence
But the vastness has sucked the air from my lungs dry.
I've been dancing dancing dancing through the stillness,
but it's getting kind of tiring,
Being so lonely in a prom dress.
I've been blazing blazing blazing through the smoke
It makes me choke, on my own blood sweat and tears.

Teen years still choking on my baby fears.
Why must I lose my baby teeth to grow my fangs?
I need to grow fangs so I can eat away my hunger pains.
My struggles sound so plain
Next to yours, yours are insane.

What's going on?
Put your glitters and smiles on.
It's time to go to prom

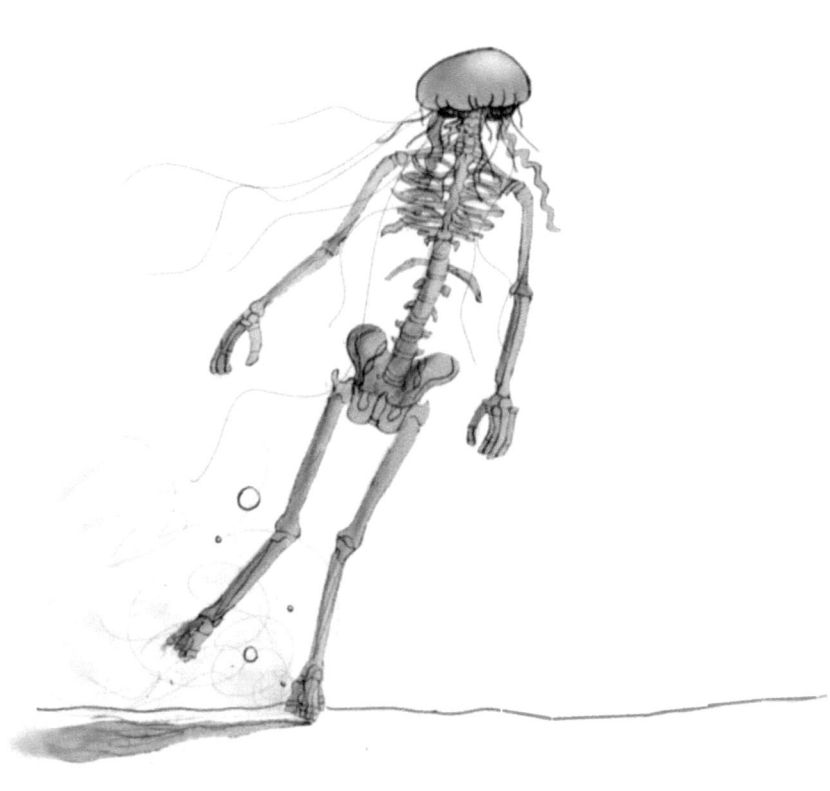

40

JELLYFISH WITH BONES

There is a jellyfish I know, that carries with it
A human's worth of bones.
The skeleton drags along on the seabed,
The jelly unable to swim off on its own.
Is he trying to help the human?
Even though he has no head?
Doesn't he know all this extra weight,
Is utterly, completely dead?

It seems quite unusual, doesn't it,
For such a delicate, complex creature
To carry such a great burden,
That was never meant for it to hold?
We would be patient with it? Wouldn't we?
Or at the very least pity it, as it drearily passes by.

But I am this creature,
And you are this creature,
We all carry these memories,
These standards, these bullies, around with us,
From when we were young and like clay,

All we wanted was to be safe, all we wanted was to play.
Our first steps, on thin ice, our first words, apologies.

And now we are dragged down to the pits of despair,
Distracting these intricate skeletons worth of problems
With playing games and taking pictures and making money
and dying our hair.

But humans were never meant to carry such traumas,
Or unreachably high ambitions,
Making our vision like cones,
It is just as unnatural for a jellyfish to have bones.

So be patient;
Not all of us,
Can just let go.

Part Five:
The Solace

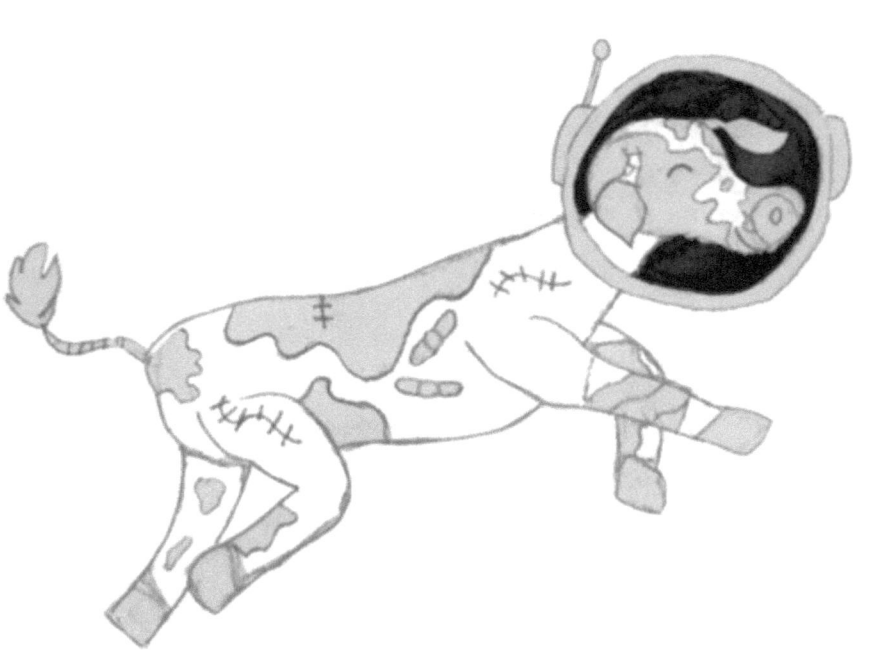

41

TREEHOUSES

There is an immense forest
That appears in the winter,
And every tree has a treehouse
That matches a child in the world,
Reflecting their personality and passions.

Children often visit their treehouses late in the night
Drifting into the snow-covered wood on a bed of dreams,
Inside they will play and learn
And befriend and explore and rest.
But as children grow up,
They often visit their treehouses less and less,
And it slowly falls into disarray,
Eventually crumbling to the ground.

Some children's treehouses crumble too soon,
At no fault of their own.
And they didn't get to play in it much, if at all.
Leaving them alone in the dirt and the cold and the rubble,
While echoes of laughter can be heard from high above.
And they wonder,

"Why don't I deserve a treehouse of my own?"

Fortunately, many of those children grow up to learn,
They do deserve a treehouse of their own.
And as adults, bruised and bandaged and healing,
They return to this forest and find their tree
And bit by bit, begin to repair what was lost.

You may get splinters along the way,
And it may end up a precarious hodgepodge of a thing.
And other adults may tease and insult you for even returning,
But it is worth it, to climb up the makeshift ladder,
And play and learn and befriend and explore and rest
In a treehouse, of your very own.

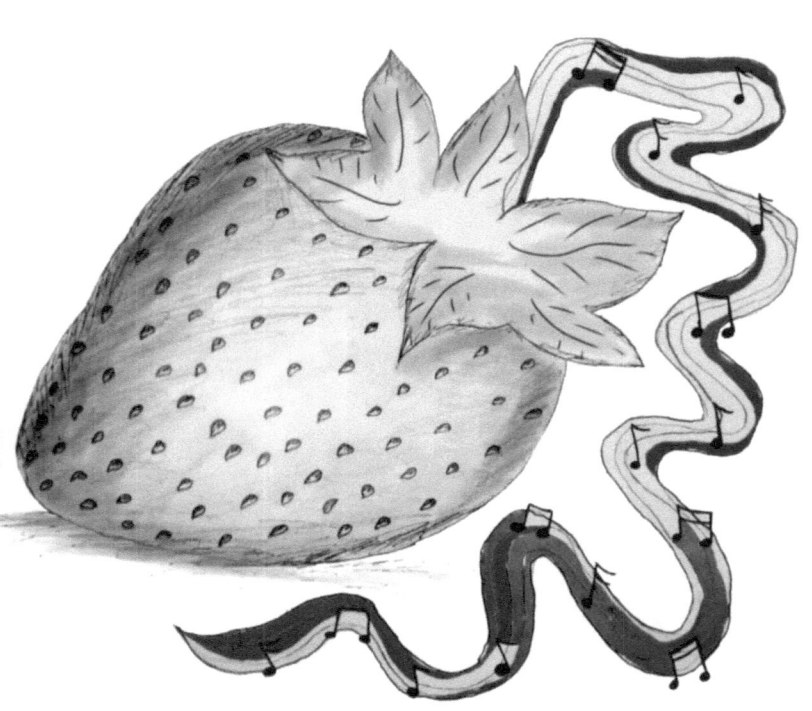

42

MELODY OF A STRAWBERRY

My mind is an alibi, created by self.
My body is a melody, composed by the Lord.
They try to work together,
To create some logic and stability.
But who am I? Who am I? Who am I?
But a strawberry on the vine,
Just passing the time,
Waiting to blossom, longing to bloom.

Hoping to be plucked from the vine,
By someone who appreciates my sweet.
Who will count my seeds, and delicately pick away my leaves.
But who already knows this strawberry inside and out?
And loves it so,
Than the Lord who composed the lyrics of my bones,
Who sang into me a breath of song and soul.
The one who made me, this melody of a strawberry.

EVENINGS

I love evenings with prayer.
And I love evenings with baths.
I love evenings with cartoons.
And I love evenings with rain.
I love evenings with blankets.
And I love evenings with laughter.
I love evenings with mac and cheese.
And I love evenings with secrets.
I love evenings with books.
And I love evenings with art.
I love evenings with stuffed animals,
And I love evenings with scary movies.
I love evenings with tea,
And I love evenings with karaoke.
I love evenings to myself.

But mostly, I love evenings with all of you.

MAGNUM OPUS

Even if life has brewed your heart
Into a monsoon,
You can raise your Magnum Opus,
To be a light bearing soul.

CAROUSEL OF MEMORY

I am always riding a carousel of memory,
Round and round,
Processing the ups and downs.

I think about happy times with friends,
Times I wish would never end.

I think about regrets,
And wonder why I was ever such a way,
I think about missed opportunities and wonder
Where I'd be today.

I think about the big events that shaped me,
It's a wonder how all of these created such a personality.

I think about times that were just a dream,
and what they could possibly mean.

And that's okay, we all need to sort things out sometimes
Memories that are hard, or memories that are fun.

But once in a while it's good to get off that fiberglass horse,
To go ride a real one.

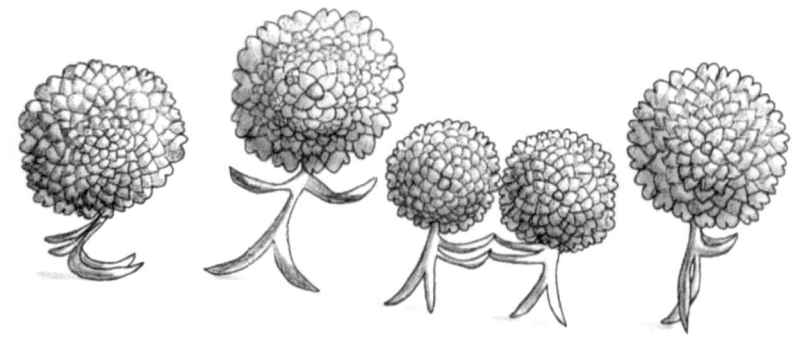

EIGHTEEN SCHOLARS

Sleep is a phantom, that refuses to haunt me
So, I let the drapes beckon me toward the window.
All is shadowed and hushed in the night,
But as my eyes adjust, the wild growth comes to life.

Crystalline curtains flare from the moon,
Reaching to and away in beams and cones.
The almost light graciously wafting down
Like the steam from boiled milk.

Beneath its ambient brilliance
My favorite flowers are growing
Their pink petals unfolding in patterned motifs
Like the copious eyes of archangels

I cock my head, and imagine them,
Fervently chanting their philosophies
Into the bittersweet night
Indulging themselves, on bittersweet wines.

I pray that mischievous Sleep will return
From the depths of its hiding place
But until then I let myself simmer in my own longing
Watching the Eighteen Scholars grow in my yard.

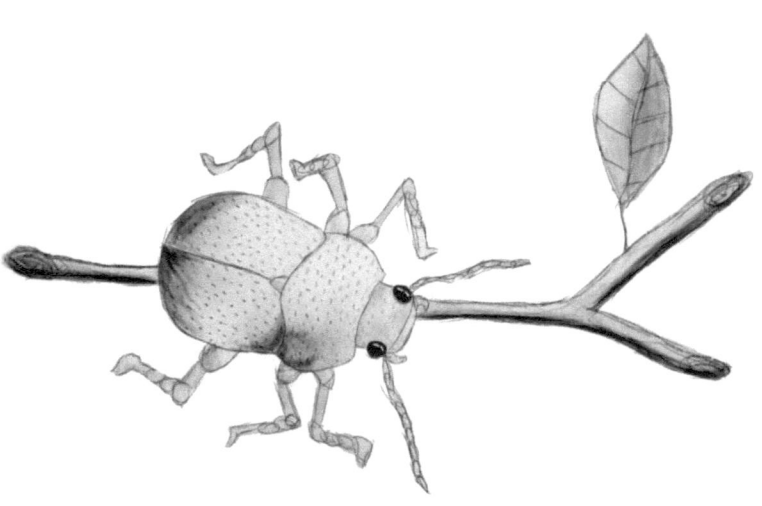

BELONG

Beetles belong among the leaf litter
And fireflies belong to the night
And bees belong over gardens
And dogs belong by our sides
And cats belong on our laps
And sheep belong on the fields
And koi fish belong in the ponds
And turtles belong in the reeds
And frogs belong in the trees
And birds belong in the clouds
And music belongs in our ears
And starlight belongs in our eyes

And I belong here;
Happy, and healthy.
And I can't let my mind tell me otherwise.

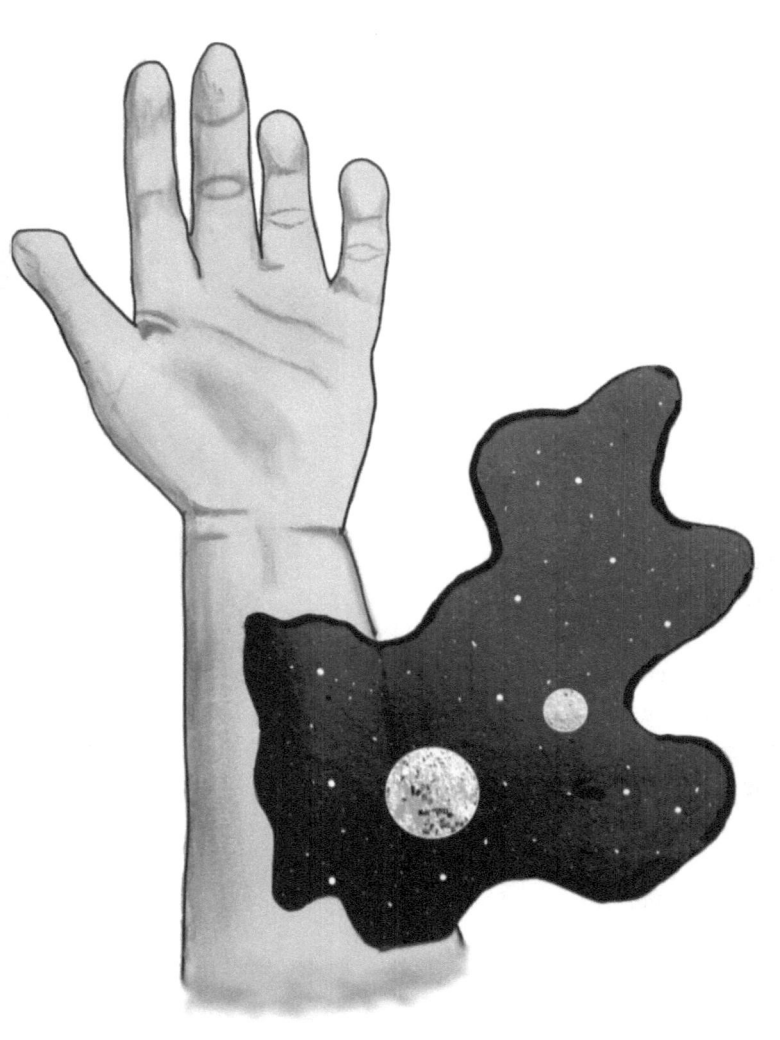

48

THE ATOMS IN ME

God did not thread my fibers
With some spare change
At the bottom of a purse,
He made me with the same precious atoms
As the universe.

Who am I
To deny
The atoms in me to flicker and flourish?

How could I be
So vain
To not give my atoms a chance
To experience and explain?

Where else would they go
If I destroyed their vessel?

How could they swim in lakes, or dance in the kitchen, or stroll
through the woods, or dream of flying, or laugh with their
friends, or eat their favorite meal, or have their first kiss, or

conquer their fears, or reach their goals, or learn something new, or add to their collections, or pray to God, or travel to another land, or pet fluffy animals, or plant gardens, or hug their family, or feel anything at all,

If I bled them all out onto the floor?

49

MY DREAM?

I want to get lost on the cobblestone streets of a city,
With a big map in my hands.
I want to ride a train through the mountains.
I want to go to art galleries. And theaters.
And libraries. And arcades. And restaurants.
Oh, I've got so many plans,
I want to snorkel, off the Gulf
I want to sing praises in different Halls
And pray with different congregations.
Oh, I am one hungry wolf,
I want to learn the country's language.
And its music. And its food. And its culture.
I want a local to lean in close and tell me
"We have a little saying around here that goes:"
And it's a quote that changes my world view forever.
Before death encircles me like a vulture;
I want to befriend its people. And its stray cats.
And its farm animals.
I want to ride my bike over rolling hills.
I want to have a picnic in the grass,
Reading a book that *I* wrote.

There's more I want, more than I can emote
I want to kiss at the top of a Ferris wheel,
And get proposed to with a *pink* stoned ring.
And get married in one of those
Big botanical garden green houses.
There's so much to do, this is only the gist,
And the globe is not just a sphere, it is a checklist

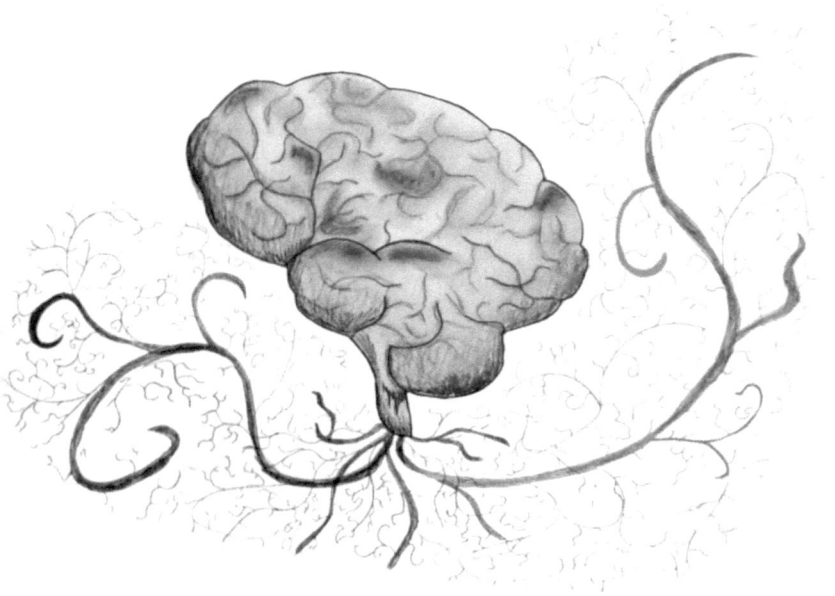

ON THE SPECTRUM

My brain has never been in tuned with the usual humdrum,
And I got diagnosed with being on the Spectrum.

So, our neurons may be flashing different codes,
And our operating systems, may be set to different modes,

We may dream in different colors,
And think on different planes,

We may communicate differently,
But our hearts are the same.

We perceive the little details,
At different angles,

And process the big picture
At different speeds.

We may have different passions,
Or entirely different needs.

But you don't have to feel sorry for me,
Or praise me as some sort of intellectual anomaly.

Just let me rest,
When my senses are putting me to the test.

Just let me feel,
When the world around me is so dazzling, it's almost unreal.

Just let me stim,
When my body wants to move in a rhythmic whim.

Just let me steal away into the night,
When the crowds around me are a fright.

I promise I want to connect,
Even if I'm not good at pleasantries and formalities.

But please,
Just be my friend,

Not my bully, or my savior.
And I promise you, we won't seem so different in the end.

But we *are* a little different, in fascinating ways,
That's not a bad thing, no matter what some skeptics say.

The world needs different perspectives and skill sets.
For solving different problems, and bringing some variety.

But remember, intelligence and talents do not measure worth.
So even if my interests don't seem useful to you,

Or my needs are at a greater level,

Do not revel, in confusion.

You don't necessarily need,
to *understand*,

In order to *accept*,
That just because my brain developed differently,

Doesn't mean I am lesser than,
Or greater than the rest.

I have found peace within myself,
And I'm excited to find adventure, everywhere else~

AFTERWORD

Thank you for reading!

ABOUT THE AUTHOR

Is this part really necessary? Can't I just remain a mystery? An enigma, if you will? The vague shadowy echo of a cryptid's whisper, wrapped in ambiguity and deep fried in *secrets.... No?* Okay, um…. My favorite color is pink :)